The Right Left HAND

And Other Poems That Will Tickle Your Brain!

written by **Vickie Thomas**

illustrated by **Charles Vesperman**

The Right Left Hand
© 2023 by Vickie Thomas

These books are available at special discounts when purchased in bulk for use as premiums, promotions, fundraising, or schools. For inquiries and details, contact us: info@gypsyheartpress.com.

Published by Gypsy Heart Press
College Station, Texas

Library of Congress Number: 2023947717
Hardback ISBN: 978-1-950714-32-2
Paperback ISBN: 978-1-950714-33-9

Contents

A note from the author . . .

I wrote these poems with the intention of reading them aloud with children. Idioms and homonyms can be a challenge for young readers and English learners, but the right voice inflection and visuals make these fun words easier to understand. I hope you enjoy many *aha* moments as you read this book with the children in your life.

—Vickie Thomas
Poet, Mama, Nanna, and Grammy

Just a Thinking

I like lying on the grass;
I do my thinking there.
Especially when it's sunny out,
And springtime's in the air.

I like smelling springtime flowers,
Even if I sneeze.
I'm fascinated following ants
While crawling on my knees.

Why does one cloud bring the rain,
Yet another's full of hail?
And some critters live in a hole in the ground,
While some critters live in a shell?

How do birds know which way's south
To get away from the snow?
And how do they know it's time to fly north?
Is it when the hot breezes blow?

Why can we hear dogs as they bark
But not hear the bark on the trees?
How can some plants eat insects,
Yet other insects eat leaves?

Maybe someday I will learn
The answers that are missing,
But for today, I think I'll grab
My cane pole and go fishing!

Icky Idioms

When someone's in a hurry—
   we say, "Get on the stick."
Or when they're going to get a swat—
   we say they'll "get a lick"!
And if they get into a fight—
   some say they're "in the thick."
And if you understand this poem—
   that means, for you, "it *clicks*"!

3

In a Pickle

I like dill pickles. Oh yes, I do!
I like crisp bread-and-butter pickles too!

I like sweet jelly, and I like tart jam.
But there's just one thing I don't understand . . .

When people get stuck in a bad situation,
What makes them think to establish the relation
Of being *in a pickle* or being *in a jam*?
Why not *in an onion* or maybe *in a yam*?!

4

Playing Possum

Miss Jones looks like a possum
    with her nose up in the air.
She has a long and pointy face
    and quite a lot of hair.
With beady eyes and tiny ears
    and bright red lipstick on,
When she gets mad and hisses,
    you will wish that you were gone!

Funny Bunnies

Flop ears, lop ears,
Standing-high-on-top ears.
Long feet, skinny toes,
Cutest little button nose.
Jackrabbits, Easter bunnies,
Cottontails, oh, so funny.
Seen 'em all, but tell me, please,
What in the world are dust bunnies?

Pennies, Pennies, Pennies

One day, this boy was thinking,
All lost inside his head,
Keeping mostly to himself,
When his teacher said . . .

"A penny for your thoughts, young man?"
So he held out his hand.
Pretty soon, he realized
He did not understand.

"Tell me what you're thinking,"
She smiled and clarified.
"I'm sure I have no thoughts up there,"
The little boy denied.

Rainy Day

I'm so glad it's pouring rain!
I thought, *I'll go catch frogs.*
But then I heard my mother say,
"It's raining cats and dogs!"

"Yippee!" I said. They must be free!
I wonder what I'll catch.
I hope a pup so I can teach
My dog to *sit* and *fetch*.

8

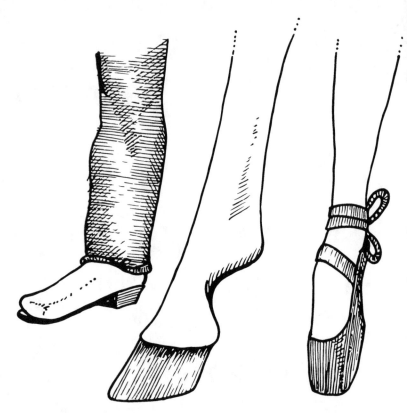

Getting a Leg Up

My neighbor's so confusing;
I don't know what he means.
But when he says to "*shake a leg*,"
It means go fast, it seems!

But when he says, "*I pulled your leg*,"
And he's not touchin' me,
It means he told some big ol' joke;
And then he slaps his knee!

One day, he bought some groceries—
He was out of steak and eggs.
My mouth fell open when he said,
"*It cost an arm and a leg*!"

9

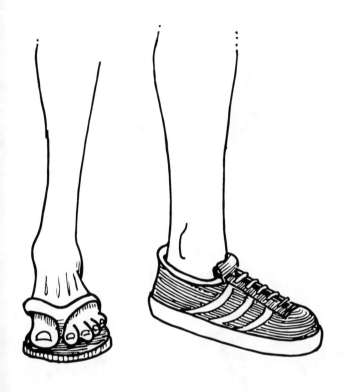

I guess I looked quite puzzled,
So he offered to explain.
Said he could give me a *"leg up"*
And make his meaning plain.

"Today is *on its last legs*,"
He said. "I'm feeling wonky.
But you can stay and chat 'cause I
Talk hind legs off of donkeys."

What? No legs on donkeys?
I did not want to see!
So don't you know I ran home fast
As my legs could carry me?

Things You
Can Scrape

When there's food left on your plate,
Don't *scrape* it in the sink.
It might go down the drain, and then
It'd really start to stink!

And if you're riding on your bike
And accidentally tumble,
You'd probably *scrape* both of your knees,
And that would make you grumble.

If you live where it's real cold,
A blizzard might blow in.
Then you'd have to *scrape* your drive
So you could leave again!

Teachers tell you, "Study hard.
There's going to be a test."
If you manage to *scrape* by,
At least you did your best!

I could go on with things you scrape,
But I've run out of paper.
Still, I'm wondering, who can tell me,
What is a *skySCRAPER*?

Hom-i-ny
and
Hom-o-nyms

I love to eat some hom-i-ny;
It kind of tastes like corn.
So I got real excited when
I got to school this morn'.

Teacher said, "You're going to learn
A thing called hom-o-nyms."
I figured she meant hom-i-ny,
so I clapped and yelled, "Amen!"

Oh, life is so confusing.
Those hom-o-nyms, it seems,
Are words that sound and spell the same
But mean two different things.

Like train a dog or ride a train;
Don't lie, but let the cat lie.
Or fly the skies in a big airplane,
But *never* swallow a blow*fly*!

The RIGHT Left Hand

Tommy left and went inside
The building on the right.
"He left?" asked he.
"That's right," said I,
"He had to go and write."

"But his hand is in a cast.
"It's broken, is that true?"
"That's right, he broke his right hand,
So the left will have to do."

"But that's the wrong one! Can he learn
To write with the left?" asked he.
"It may be wrong, but it can become
The right left hand," says me!

13

Katydid

Katy Petty swallowed a bug—
It made the kids all giggle.
But then she started turning green;
Her body shook and wiggled.
Next thing you know, she sprouted wings,
And flew away, she did!
Who knew eating bugs was cool?
Well, I guess Katydid!

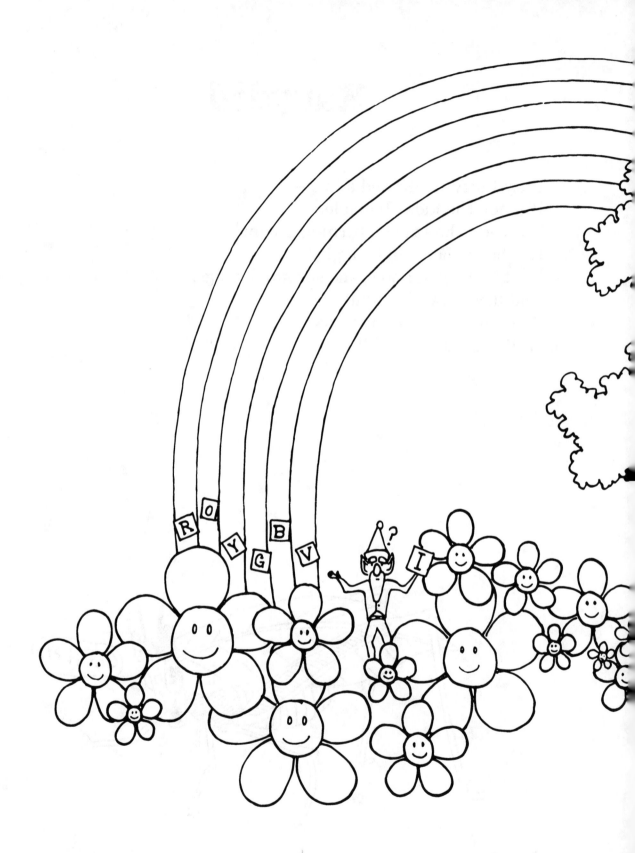

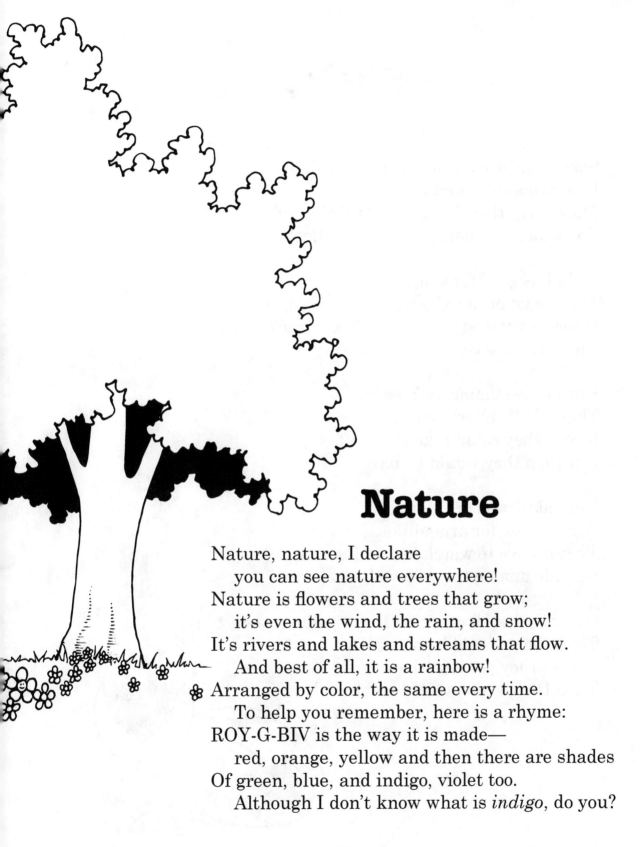

Nature

Nature, nature, I declare
   you can see nature everywhere!
Nature is flowers and trees that grow;
   it's even the wind, the rain, and snow!
It's rivers and lakes and streams that flow.
   And best of all, it is a rainbow!
Arranged by color, the same every time.
   To help you remember, here is a rhyme:
ROY-G-BIV is the way it is made—
   red, orange, yellow and then there are shades
Of green, blue, and indigo, violet too.
   Although I don't know what is *indigo*, do you?

16

Shells

Some creatures have super hard shells,
Like armadillos and turtles.
They carry their houses on their backs'
You won't see them jumping hurdles!

A shell is good for self-defense.
They've no need to be wary
Unless they're stuck on a railroad track
And a train is coming—that's scary!

But in the summer, it's so hot!
Their shells allow no air.
If only they could take them off,
But then they would be bare!

Nekkid turtles are a sight;
Same's true for armadillos.
They'd have to watch for sunburn or
Go hide among the willows!

Or slather each other with super sunscreen;
Then there would be no worries.
Unless they got it in their eyes,
Then their vision would be blurry!

My First Transformer

I had a little fishy; he swam in a dish,
I wanted just to watch him become a *bigger* fish!
I checked on his water, gave him stuff to eat.
But, boy, was I surprised when he started growing feet!

First it was two legs, then it was four.
I was really kinda scared he might grow some more.
But days went by, and I'da bet you a quarter,
Old fishy's tail was getting shorter and shorter!

And then one day, I heard a croaking sound.
My little fish was nowhere to be found.
But there was a frog, sittin' in the corner.
"It's a miracle, Mom! I created a transformer!"

Creepy Crawlies

Bug is such a tiny word;
Let's call them "creepy crawlies."
Because they come in every size—
From short to big and tall-ies.

Some on the ground, some in the air,
Crawling slow or flying quickly,
Some soft with slimy outerwear,
Others hard and rather prickly.

They're still just bugs and fun to watch,
Like ants and worms and beetles.
And ladybugs with their red and black,
But I'll *never* like mosquitos!!

Wait for meeeeeeeeeeeeeeeeeeeeeeeeeeeeee!

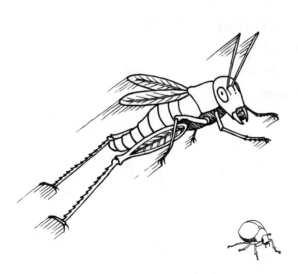

More Bugs

Roly-polies, pill bugs,
Doodlebugs, and ants,

Tiny little buggies,
Crawlin' 'round the plants!

There's probably 'bout a million of 'em
Doing a little dance.

I just hope they don't find me
And crawl right up my pants!!

The Sloth

There was a critter in a tree.
I saw him, and he saw me.
'Cept he was upside down, you see,
This furry, three-toed sloth.

His arms and legs were lean and long,
And when he swam, he was oh so strong!
But I knew something must be wrong
With this furry, three-toed sloth.

'Cause all day long he hung upside down—
When he ate, when he slept—with his claws wrapped 'round
A tree, and his fur full of ticks crawlin' 'round.
This furry three-toed sloth.

I think when it's time to select a pet,
A sloth could be quite unique, and yet
If hanging head-down is as good as it gets,
I might just get a dog.

How Hot Was It?

I guess it was hot in church today.
The preacher was really on fire!
And people were sweating bullets, they said—
Especially the ones in the choir.

At the final "amen," we ran out the doors,
Gasping, beginning to cough.
I sure am glad that no one saw
My skunk in the choir loft!

Adventureland

Today we went to Adventureland;
It's like a backwards zoo.
You stay in the car with your windows down,
And the animals look at you!

We watched as Mama gave food to a llama
Then turned to tug my hair.
"Say hi to the 'ena," said Mom
When she seen a hyena, just standing there.

H·NORKEN!

23

"Ooh, look, there's an efalant coming this way;
You think we can pet his trunk?"
But the efalant sneezed and fell on his knees
And blew out a trunk-full of junk!

We never went back to Adventureland,
And that's just fine with me.
I'd just as soon not be around
If an efalant has to sneeze!

24

Plastic

My parents have a credit card—
It's just a piece of plastic.

But it can get you anything
For free; it's just fantastic!

I called the store and ordered up
A birthday gift for Mama.

She will sure be so surprised
When she gets her new llama!

Where Do Babies Come From?

"Where do babies come from?"
"From eggs," I told my friend.
"And then the baby breaks the shell,
And the mama starts again."

"It's all a kind of guessing game—
What baby will appear.
Could be a turtle or a chick;
Could be a baby deer."

"Which reminds me that my mom
Will have a baby soon.
I sure hope when her egg breaks,
It will be a baby 'coon!"

The Monster in My Room

Mama read a story, then she tucked me into bed.
She wrapped the blanket 'round me, nothing showing but my head.

Pretty soon, I nodded off; it was so still and quiet.
I woke up to an eerie sound that broke the silent night.

I could not move, so scared was I, eyes darting all around,
Trying to identify the scary, frightful sound.

Shining eyes stared back at me; I knew the thing was close.
Could it be a monster? An animal? A ghost?

Maybe it's a dream, I thought and squeezed my eyes so tight.
And when I opened them again, the sun was shining bright!

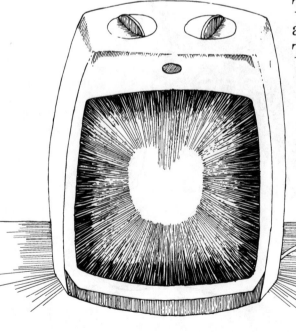

The monster blew its warming breath,
and then I turned and saw—
The heater with the glowing eyes
   was no monster at all!

Sewer's Ditch

I like to go to grandma's house; there's always stuff to do.
We run barefoot everywhere; don't have to wear no shoes!

One day, Grandma says to us, "Don't go near that ditch,
'Cause if you slip and fall in it, I'm gonna get my switch!"

Now don't you know, I jumped it still—and was not even close.
I popped up green and gagging 'cause that sewer smelled so
gross!

For me, I learned a lesson. And it didn't take a switch!
Listen to your grandma when she warns you 'bout that ditch!

The Sad Suitor

Young Charlie felt faint and quite dizzy,
When he saw the cute blonde-haired girl, Lizzy.
His stomach did lurch,
And he threw up in church!
Not likely to woo her now, is he?

Fuzz

On the floor, a piece of fuzz—
Yessiree, that's what it was.
I picked it up and threw it down.
I didn't want that thing around.

The trash can is the place for you!
Don't want you sticking to my shoe
Or flying up all in my food!
A piece of fuzz is just so crude!

The Knock

As I was lying on the floor,
I heard a knock upon my door.
I did not want to go and see
Just who had come to visit me.

But when the knocks grew loud and clear,
I knew that I could never hear
Or concentrate on what I read.
It just flew in and out my head!

I then got up and went to see
Just who had come to visit me.
But when I made it to the door,
I found that they were there no more!

Boogers

Boogers in my nose.
There's *boogers* in my nose!
Every single morning—
This is how it goes.
First, I get a tissue;
I blows and blows and blows.
But all I get is snot, you see,
That flows and flows and flows!

Sometimes I get to digging.
(I hope nobody knows.)
But still, I feel them up there,
These boogers in my nose.
I wiggle, and I waggle
My face in every pose.
Tryin' hard to loosen up
Those boogers in my nose.

I blow so hard it seems as if
I'm blowing from my toes!
When out flies that old booger,
Forceful as a fire hose!
Breaks right through the tissue,
And lands right on my clothes!
Is anybody watching?
Now, what do you suppose?!

Misery

I can't go to school today;
I'm really, really sick.
I need another day of rest,
And that might do the trick!

My head is super stuffy.
There's a pain behind my eye.
My nose is plugged, and I can't breathe.
Feels like I'm gonna die.

Someone call a doctor,
A nurse or paramedic.
Someone take my temperature;
I think I'm diabetic!

"Mom, come quick," I groan aloud.
"No school for me today!"
"Of course there's not, you silly boy.
Today is *Saturday*!"

33

The Haircut

I cut my hair this morning,
   and Mommy was so proud!
You should have heard her when she saw
   and cheered so very loud!
I really did a good job;
   now I can see my ears!
Guess that explains why she looks at me
   and her eyes fill up with tears.
She must be even prouder
   than I was even guessing
Because I heard her praying,
   "Give me strength to endure my blessings!"

Conquerors!

I like to play computer games
With action, lights, and sounds.
And guide the mighty warriors as
They fight each challenge round.

Facing *greegs* and dodging *wogs*,
We have to save the world!
Let's send these troublemakers back
To where all snakes are curled.

To a land of fire and darkness,
Far from the light of day.
While we, the mighty warriors,
Live to fight another day!

S'Mores

Written by the author's granddaughter Madison Brooke McCleary

Ooey-gooey, drippy, chewy
Chocolate goodness melting down my chin.
Toasted marshmallows, golden brown,
Golden cracker wrapped around.
Ahh, the perfect sandwich!
Give us s'more! Give us s'more!

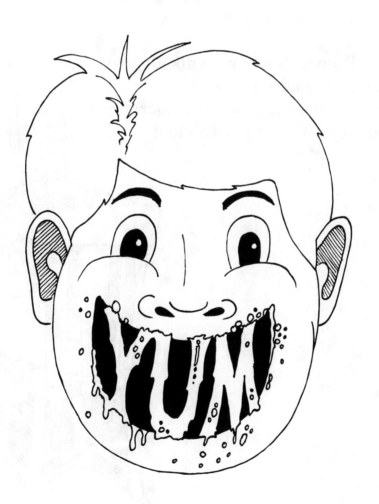

Checkers

Mr. Brown and Mr. Grump
Played checkers every day.
And Grump would always cheat as soon
As Brown would look away.

"You know what happens when you cheat?"
Scowled Brown, his face affright!
"The Gadzooks come up from the ground
And torment you all night!"

With that, Brown stood and walked away.
Poor Grump, he had no clue—
That Brown came early just this morn'
And filled Grump's chair with glue!

Number Sense

I am the best at numbers
The world has ever seen!
I can already count to ten with only
A short pause in between.
Next I'll tackle the alphabet.
I'm sure I will have no trouble
Learning all my Ps and Qs,
And all my Vs and Doubles.

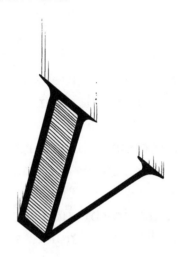

Screech

Oh. My. Goodness! What is that awful noise?
It sounds like someone's fighting—like cats or maybe boys?

Someone call Emergency! Tell them hurry! *Quick*!
I hear groans and howling now. Someone might be sick!

I rush in through my front door with all my superpower!
And find the noise is just my brother, singing in the shower!

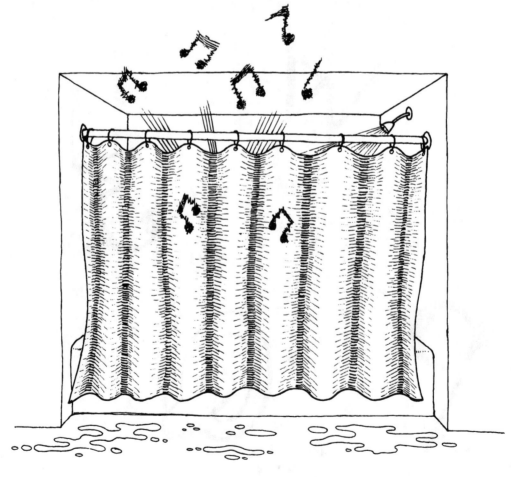

Curmudgeon

Mama called me a *curmudgeon*!
I don't think it's fair that she's judgin'!
I'm cranky and mad—
But only half bad.
That's my story, and, Mom, I ain't budgin'!

Kindness

Sometimes, a person might stutter,
And someone yells, "Just spit it out!"
Well, it's not like they swallowed a
    seed, you know.
That's not what it's all about.

I think a much better option
Would be to keep your mouth closed,
And wait for the other to finish!
Isn't that the way kindness goes?!

Looking Good

Mama likes to paint her face
    with stuff she calls her "potions."
There's powders, creams, and colored sticks,
    and even smelly lotions.
She says it helps her hide her flaws,
    her little "imperfections."
I don't know why it bothers her
    when I play with her collections.
But I really need to fix my face,
    'Cause tonight I have a date
To the daddy-daughter dance,
    and you know we can't be late!
Eye shadow here, lipstick there,
    and some color on my cheek.
"Ready, Dad, so here I come.
    Close your eyes. Don't peek!"
I beam with pride when Daddy grins
    and says, "Come let me kiss you."
Then he gently bends and wipes my face
    with a little bit of tissue.
"All perfect now," my dad declares.
    "My girl is just so clever!"
And I know that this will be
    the very best night ever!

An American

"What is an American?" my teacher asked today.
"I think it is the president," I heard somebody say.

"Someone from California?" came a question from the back.
"I think it is the flag we fly or a picture on a plaque."

"What about a soldier who wears camo every day?
Who fights for freedom and protects the good old USA?"

The teacher smiled, her eyes so bright.
"Well, dear class, you all are right!

"Americans are people, just like me and just like you.
Who treasure all the freedoms of our great red, white, and blue.

"Who pledge faithful allegiance to the flag for which it stands
And promise to uphold the Constitution of this land.

"Who celebrate diversity in this great melting pot
Of people from around the world, in word and deed and thought."

When I Grow Up

When I grow up, I'll be the boss,
Tell others what to do!
And if I say I'm hungry now,
They'll have to bring me food!

When I am grown, I won't have to
Go home and take a bath.
I'll never have to go to school
'Cause big kids don't need math!

When I grow up, I'll play all day
And never clean my room.
I won't have to brush my teeth
Or learn to use a broom!

Yes, someday I'll be all grown up,
No longer a beginner!
But, Mom, if you don't mind right now,
Would you please make me dinner?

Grandpa's Swing

Grandpa has a front-yard swing
   hanging in a tall pine tree.
And every time we visit him,
   he always pushes me.
Up and back, to and fro,
   and sometimes in a spin.
I get so dizzy, still I say,
   "Hey, Grandpa, do it again!"
So up, up, up, I go again
   until I'm soaring high!
Says Grandpa, "Someday soon, my girl,
   someday, you'll touch the sky!"

Pappah

My pappah loves me, this I know,
'cause each and every time I go
to see him, we have so much fun,
from early morn to setting sun.

We get up early before it's hot
and drive the tractor Pappah bought
to trim the grass or take a ride,
and then we go and play inside.

Building forts with blankets and sheets
tossed over chairs. Right under we creep,
fighting off bad guys, calm and steady,
until we hear Mammah—"C'mon, lunch is ready!"

And then Pappah watches me ride on my bike,
millions of miles, and then we will hike
to the end of the driveway to pick up our mail
and then to the garden with clippers and pail.
We gather hot peppers and bright red tomatoes,
okra and squash, and some sweet potatoes.

My pappah loves me, this I know,
'cause of all the ways he shows.
I'll do these things when I am grown
and have lots of kids and grandkids of my own!

F is for...

G is for...

Grandmothers

Do you know what a grandma is?
It's a little old lady who doesn't have kids.
She does not work and has plenty of time
To make me cookies, Play-Doh, and slime.
She has dishes to play in the sand,
And drums and kazoos to make a band.
At lunch, she has my favorite things,
Like pizza and corn dogs, fried onion rings!
And when it is time for grandma to nap,
She gets a good book, pulls me up in her lap.
We rock in her rocker while time fades away.
This is my favorite time of the day.

Thick and Thin

"How much do you love me, Mom?"
Asked the child one winter's night.
"I love you more than all the sun
And moon and stars so bright!"

"What if I outgrow your lap,
And we can't fit in your chair?"
"Then we'll spread a blanket on the ground,
And I'll sing to you right there!"

"And when I'm big and go to school,
What will happen then?"
"I'll pack your lunch and send you off,
Then pick you up again!"

"Through thick and thin, good times and bad,
From morn' 'til day is done,
I'll always be your mama, and
You'll always be my son!"

Best Life

Remember the woman who lived in a shoe?
  There are places I'd much rather live, and you?
Like maybe a yacht, a skiff, or canoe,
  just floating on water and fishing some too!
Or maybe, just maybe, if I had a whim,
  I'd jump overboard and take me a swim!
Splishing and splashing 'til the sun would grow dim,
  and all I could see on horizon's far rim
Was a sky painted orange, red, yellow, and pink—
  that would be my favorite place, I think!

Printed in the USA
CPSIA information can be obtained
at www.ICGtesting.com
LVHW081614141123
763661LV00012B/570